SHAMBHALA
CLASSICS

The Book of Tea

KAKUZO OKAKURA

Introduction by
SAM HAMILL

SHAMBHALA
Boston & London · 2001

SHAMBHALA PUBLICATIONS, INC.
Horticultural Hall
300 Massachusetts Avenue
Boston, Massachusetts 02115
www.shambhala.com

Cover photo and plates courtesy of Bishin Jumonji,
used with permission.
Introduction © 2001 by Sam Hamill.

9 8 7 6 5 4 3 2 1

Printed in the United States of America
 ∞ This edition is printed on acid-free paper that meets
the American National Standards Institute z39.48 Standard.
Distributed in the United States by Random House, Inc.,
and in Canada by Random House of Canada Ltd

The Library of Congress catalogues the previous edition of this book as follows:
Okakura, Kakuzō, 1862–1913
The book of tea / Kakuzo Okakura.
—1st Shambhala ed.
p. cm. — (Shambhala pocket classics)
ISBN 0-87773-918-8 (alk. paper)
ISBN 1-57062-828-9 (pbk.)
1. Japanese tea ceremony.   I. Title.   II. Series.
GT2910.06 1993   92-50737
394.1'5 — dc20   CIP

Contents

Introduction

In one of the most often quoted passages in Japanese literature, the poet Basho wrote at the beginning
of his *Knapsack Notebook*:

> Saigyo in poetry, Sogi in linked verse, Sesshu in
> painting, Rikyu in the tea ceremony—the spirit
> that moves them is one spirit. Achieving artistic
> excellence, each holds one attribute in common:
> each remains attuned to nature throughout the
> four seasons. Whatever is seen by such a heart
> and mind is a flower, whatever is dreamed is a
> moon. Only a barbarian mind could fail to see

the flower; only an animal mind could fail to dream a moon. The first task for each artist is to overcome the barbarian or animal heart and mind, to become one with nature.

At a glance it may seem peculiar to the Western mind that one of Japan's greatest poets would equate the simple tea ceremony with the best classical verse and painting. It's not exactly like comparing a perfect latte with an exquisite painting by Morris Graves or Van Gogh, but the comparison serves to present Zen mind at its best. One may address any art form by considering "right mindfulness" and "right practice" essential to any art; thus, the art of making coffee and the art of painting are direct expressions of mindfulness and practice. The "simplicity" of the tea ceremony is as complex as the richest painting or poem, and like painting and poetry, the ceremony draws upon centuries of tradition in order to arrive at what is fully present. Nearly a hundred years ago, Okakura Kakuzo wrote:

Those of us who know not the secret of properly regulating our own existence on this tumultuous sea of foolish troubles which we call life are constantly in a state of misery while vainly trying to appear happy and contented. We stagger in the attempt to keep our moral equilibrium, and see forerunners of the tempest in every cloud that floats on the horizon. Yet there is joy and beauty in the roll of the billows as they sweep outward toward eternity. Why not enter into their spirit, or, like Liehtse, ride upon the hurricane itself? He only who has lived with the beautiful can die beautifully.

To "die beautifully" is to makes one's life a part of a greater work of art. "Beauty and ugliness have origins," Lao Tzu warns, and they are less a matter of received opinion than a consequence of acting upon whatever is already within each of us. While Western materialist culture declares that certain paintings are worth millions of dollars, Zen reminds us that the masterpiece is temporal, and that Hui Neng (638–713), the sixth patriarch of Zen, expressed his enlightenment by burning an image of the Awakened One. Zen mind rings with quiet laughter. "Have a cup of tea!" Or, "Paint the sound of the wind in the pines!"

Speaking of art appreciation, Okakura writes, "Our mind is the canvas on which the artists lay their colour; their pigments are our emotions; their chiaroscuro the light of joy, the shadow of sadness. The masterpiece is of ourselves, as we are of the masterpiece. The sympathetic communion of minds necessary for art appreciation must be based on mutual concession. The spectator must cultivate the proper attitude for receiving the message, as the artist must know to impart it." The artist, the painting, and its audience are not three things, but one.

The founder of the Shingon Buddhist sect and one of the earliest importers of Chinese tea seeds, Kukai (774–835), taught that Buddhism contained all of the essential elements of both Taoism and Confucianism, and he made the tea ceremony an expression of nature in an evanescent existence. Yet despite his interest, the tea ceremony remained an obscure Buddhist practice for several hundred more years. Kukai was a renowned artist, calligrapher, and Sanskrit scholar, whose view of Buddhism was simultaneously scholarly and religious. He insisted upon learning directly from the Sanskrit in order achieve the "true word" (*shingon*), containing absolute truth. Other forms of Buddhism, he believed, treated only "illnesses of the mind." For Kukai, tea was probably considered a healthful and good ceremonial drink, but his religious practice was rooted in study, not in simple ceremony.

Zen, born in the interaction of Buddhism with Taoism in sixth century China, was said to be "transmission outside scripture—no dependence upon written words; pointing directly within, seeing one's own nature, attaining Buddhahood." The practice of sitting meditation eliminates dualistic thinking such as subject/object or true/false. Hui Neng insisted upon "silent, solitary self-illumination," and advocated *shikantaza,* or "sitting" as the key. Zen, then, remains much more a school of philosophy than a conventional religion. And that certainly has been a part of its appeal in the West: one may practice Zen while remaining a devout Jew, Catholic, or atheist. There is no religious conflict because the practice of Zen does not address whether or not there is a god, nor does it pass judgment on religious texts. Zen mind is "ordinary everyday mind," and the tea ceremony is, like sweeping the garden or planting rice or working at a desk, refined but commonplace, a ritual performed not as an emblem, but as useful in and of itself. Bringing Zen mind to the task at hand, every detail of every task becomes simple and luminous. The tea ceremony becomes art, a ceremony performed not as symbol or allegory, but as an ultimate expression of the here-and-now in which Zen practice is rooted. In many ways, tea mind resembles Basho's advice to poets, "Learn all the rules, then forget them." He doesn't mean to throw out the rules of composition; rather, he means to learn the tradition so thoroughly that one becomes at one with tradition. For Basho, haiku mind, tea mind, and painting mind are all merely aspects of Zen practice—the consciousness of the artist opened through years of sitting daily.

In the twelfth century, the Zen monk Eisai, founder of the Rinzai Zen sect (named after Lin Chi, d. 866), returned from studying Buddhism in China and planted tea seeds on the temple grounds. He wrote Japan's first tea book, *Kissa yoji-ki* (*Drinking Tea for Health*), and became the man most often credited with beginning the tea industry. Although Eisai did much to promote tea, once again the tea ceremony apparently did not take hold except in early Rinzai monasteries. Today, we know that many of Eisai's claims for the healthfulness of green tea have proven true. Modern research suggests it helps prevent cancer, lowers cholesterol and blood sugar levels, and helps to control high blood pressure.

Still, it wasn't until Zen master Rikyu codified the tea ceremony in the fourteenth century that it became inextricably bound to Zen. The tea ceremony has remained relatively unchanged over the last 500 years. Simplicity is the rule: simple tools, simple surroundings, no noise, no unnecessary chit-chat, no clutter. Each motion requires a clear, attentive mind. The tea room or tea house avoids any note of ostentation. It is made of common materials. The tools, the table, the teapot, and the ornament—all must be humble and harmonious. The whisk is simple bamboo, the pot iron. Each part of tea practice is like the mind of the art aficionado, becoming a small part of the greater whole. A flower, twig, or scroll reflects the season, and an ink painting may contain a haiku, but there is no religious tract, no philosophy. Each gesture, like all the materials involved, is reduced to the essential.

Okakura Kakuzo was born into a merchant family in Yokohama in 1862, and he began studying English in his infancy. While studying ecomonics and law at Tokyo Imperial University in 1877, he came under the influence of Ernest Fenollosa, a Boston professor who had gone to Japan to teach political economics only to become an impassioned student of Japanese and Chinese art. The young Okakura worked dilligently with Fenollosa and a small group of fellow enthusiasts to preserve Japanese art during a frenzy of Westernization in which treasures such as the art of Hokusai and Hiroshige were destroyed. Fenollosa's notes on classical Chinese poetry, made in Tokyo with the assistance of two Japanese professors, Mori and Ariga, became the source for Ezra Pound's translations, *Cathay*, one of the most important volumes of poetry in the last century. Fenollosa and Okakura immersed themselves in classical Asian poetry and art, each teaching the other.

In 1902, on a trip to India and China, Okakura met and exchanged ideas with the Nobel poet Rabindranath Tagore, who reinforced Okakura's notions of Asian philosophy being the perfect counterpoint to Western materialism. Their conversations resulted in Okakura's first publication in English, *The Ideals of the East* (1904), shortly before he completed *The Book of Tea* in Boston, where he became Curator of the Department of Chinese and Japanese Art at the Boston Museum of Fine Arts. He spent the last years of his life traveling extensively, especially in Asia, collecting and cataloguing art until his death at Akakura Hot Springs in the Japan Alps in 1913.

Okakura Kakuzo possessed an expansive imagination and a notably eccentric manner, as well as a passion for art and learning. A century—or very nearly so—after the writing of the first Asian tea manual in America, we would do well to keep in mind the historical perspective of some of his comments. His apology for Japanese nationalism, for instance, was written at a time when Japan and Russia were quarreling and two decades before Hirohito's ascension to the throne.

"The tea room," Okakura observed, "was an oasis in the dreary waste of existence where weary travellers could meet to drink from the common spring of art-appreciation." Behind the tea ceremony, he saw the long traditions of Confucianism, Taoism, and Zen blossoming as one, including even "the ethereal aroma of Sakyamuni himself." And why was such import placed within the arena of such a brief, simple drama? "Those who cannot feel the littleness of great things in themselves,"

Okakura writes in an almost exact quotation from Confucius, "are apt to overlook the greatness of little things in others."

The Book of Tea is a classic. Nearly a hundred years after it was written, it remains the one English language masterpiece on the subject. While the author's substantial contribution to the salvation and appreciation of Asian art is largely forgotten in the West, his little book on the history and culture of tea has been read by generation after generation. But it would be foolish to think of his book as only a treatise on tea. It has and will continue to be a classic in part because of its author's insights into Confucianism, Taoism, and Zen. In Japan Okakura is still revered, known not by his family name, but simply as Tenshin, "Heaven Heart/Mind."

Sam Hamill
Kage-an, 2000

The Book of Tea

The Cup of Humanity

Tea began as a medicine and grew into a beverage. In China, in the eighth century, it entered the realm of poetry as one of the polite amusements. The fifteenth century saw Japan ennoble it into a religion of aestheticism—teaism. Teaism is a cult founded on the adoration of the beautiful among the sordid facts of everyday existence. It inculcates purity and harmony, the mystery of mutual charity, the romanticism of the social order. It is essentially a worship of the imperfect, as it is a tender attempt to accomplish something possible in this impossible thing we know as life.

The philosophy of tea is not mere aestheticism in the ordinary acceptance of the term, for it expresses conjointly with ethics and religion our whole point of view about man and nature. It is hygiene, for it enforces cleanliness; it is economics, for it shows comfort in simplicity rather than in the complex and costly; it is moral geometry, inasmuch as it defines our sense of proportion to the universe. It represents the true spirit of eastern democracy by making all its votaries aristocrats in taste.

The long isolation of Japan from the rest of the world, so conducive to introspection, has been highly favorable to the development of teaism. Our home and habits, costume and cuisine, porcelain, lacquer, painting—our very literature—all have been subject to its influence. No student of Japanese culture could ever ignore its presence. It has permeated the elegance of noble boudoirs, and entered the abode of the humble. Our peasants have learned to arrange flowers, our meanest laborer to offer his salutation to the rocks and waters. In our common parlance we speak of the man "with no tea" in him, when he is insusceptible to the seriocomic interests of the personal drama. Again we stigmatize the untamed aesthete who, regardless of the mundane tragedy, runs riot in the springtide of emancipated emotions, as one "with too much tea" in him.

The outsider may indeed wonder at this seeming much ado about nothing. "What a tempest in a teacup!" he will say. But when we consider how small after all the cup of human enjoyment is, how soon overflowed with tears, how easily drained to the dregs in our quenchless thirst for infinity, we shall not blame ourselves for making so much of the teacup. Mankind has done worse. In the worship of Bacchus, we have sacrificed too freely; and we have even transfigured the gory image of Mars. Why not consecrate ourselves to the queen of the Camellias, and revel in the warm stream of sympathy that flows from her altar? In the liquid amber within the ivory porcelain, the initiated may touch the sweet reticence of Confucius, the piquancy of Lao-tzu, and the ethereal aroma of Shakyamuni himself.

Those who cannot feel the littleness of great things in themselves are apt to overlook the greatness of little things in others. The average westerner, in his sleek complacency, will see in the tea ceremony but another instance of the thousand-and-one oddities which constitute the quaintness and childishness of the East to him. He was wont to regard Japan as barbarous while she indulged in the gentle arts of peace: he calls her civilized since she began to commit wholesale slaughter on Manchurian battlefields. Much comment has been given lately to the code of the samurai—the art of death which makes our soldiers exult in self-sacrifice; but scarcely any attention has been drawn to teaism, which represents so much of our art of life. Fain would we remain barbarians, if our claim to civilization were to be based on the gruesome glory of war. Fain would we await the time when due respect shall be paid to our art and ideals.

When will the West understand, or try to understand, the East? We Asiatics are often appalled by the curious web of facts and fancies which has been woven concerning us. We are pictured as living on the perfume of the lotus, if not on mice and cockroaches. It is either impotent fanaticism or else abject voluptuousness. Indian spirituality has been derided as ignorance, Chinese sobriety as stupidity, Japanese patriotism as the result of fatalism. It has been said that we are less sensible to pain and wounds on account of the callousness of our nervous organization!

Why not amuse yourselves at our expense? Asia

returns the compliment. There would be further food for merriment if you were to know all that we have imagined and written about you. All the glamor of the perspective is there, all the unconscious homage of wonder, all the silent resentment of the new and undefined. You have been loaded with virtues too refined to be envied, and accused of crimes too picturesque to be condemned. Our writers in the past—the wise men who knew—informed us that you had bushy tails somewhere hidden in your garments, and often dined off a fricassée of newborn babes! Nay, we had something worse against you: we used to think you the most impracticable people on the earth, for you were said to preach what you never practiced.

Such misconceptions are fast vanishing among us. Commerce has forced the European tongues on many an eastern port. Asiatic youths are flocking to western colleges for the equipment of modern education. Our insight does not penetrate your culture deeply, but at least we are willing to learn. Some of my compatriots have adopted too much of your customs and too much of your etiquette, in the delusion that the acquisition of stiff collars and tall silk hats comprised the attainment of your civilization. Pathetic and deplorable as such affectations are, they evince our willingness to approach the West on our knees. Unfortunately the western attitude is unfavorable to the understanding of the East. The Christian missionary goes to impart, but not to receive. Your information is based on the meager translations of our immense literature, if not on the unreliable anecdotes of passing travellers. It is rarely that the chivalrous pen of a Lafcadio Hearn or that of the author of *The Web of Indian Life* enlivens the oriental darkness with the torch of our own sentiments.

Perhaps I betray my own ignorance of the tea cult by being so outspoken. Its very spirit of politeness exacts that you say what you are expected to say, and no more. But I am not to be a polite teaist. So much harm has been done already by the mutual misunderstanding of the New World and the Old, that one need not apologize for contributing his tithe to the furtherance of a better understanding. The beginning of the twentieth century would have been spared the spectacle of sanguinary warfare if Russia had condescended to know Japan better. What dire consequences to humanity lie in the contemptuous ignoring of Eastern problems! European imperialism, which does not disdain to raise the absurd cry of the Yellow Peril, fails to realize that Asia may also awaken to the cruel sense of the White Disaster. You may laugh at us for having "too much tea," but may we not suspect that you of the West have "no tea" in your constitution?

Let us stop the continents from hurling epigrams at each other, and be sadder if not wiser by the mutual gain of half a hemisphere. We have developed along different lines, but there is no reason why one should not supplement the other. You have gained expansion at the cost of restlessness; we have created a harmony which is weak against aggression. Will you believe it?—the East is better off in some respects than the West!

Strangely enough humanity has so far met in the teacup. It is the only Asiatic ceremonial which commands universal esteem. The white man has scoffed at our religion and our morals, but has accepted the brown beverage without hesitation. The afternoon tea is now an important function in western society. In the delicate clatter of trays and saucers, in the soft rustle of feminine hospitality, in the common catechism about cream and sugar, we know that the worship of tea is established beyond question. The philosophic resignation of the guest to the fate awaiting him in the dubious decoction proclaims that in this single instance the oriental spirit reigns supreme.

, , ,

The earliest record of tea in European writing is said to be found in the statement of an Arabian traveller, that after the year 879 the main sources of revenue in Canton were the duties on salt and tea. Marco Polo records the deposition of a Chinese minister of finance in 1285 for his arbitrary augmentation of the tea taxes. It was at the period of the great discoveries that the European people began to know more about the extreme Orient. At the end of the sixteenth century the Hollanders brought the news that a pleasant drink was made in the East from the leaves of a bush. The travellers Giovanni Batista Ramusio (1559), L. Almeida (1576), Maffeno (1588), Tareira (1610), also mentioned tea. In the last-named year ships of the Dutch East India Company brought the first tea into Europe. It was known in France in 1636, and reached Russia in 1638. England welcomed it in 1650 and spoke of it as "That excellent and by all physicians approved

China drink, called by the Chineans Tcha, and by other nations Tay, alias Tee."

Like all the good things of the world, the propaganda of tea met with opposition. Heretics like Henry Saville (1678) denounced drinking it as a filthy custom. Jonas Hanway (*Essay on Tea*, 1756) said that men seemed to lose their stature and comeliness, women their beauty through the use of tea. Its cost at the start (about fifteen or sixteen shillings a pound) forbade popular consumption, and made it "regalia for high treatments and entertainments, presents being made thereof to princes and grandees." Yet in spite of such drawbacks tea drinking spread with marvellous rapidity. The coffee houses of London in the early half of the eighteenth century became, in fact, tea houses, the resort of wits like Addison and Steele, who beguiled themselves over their "dish of tea." The beverage soon became a necessary of life—a taxable matter. We are reminded in this connection what an important part it plays in modern history. Colonial America resigned herself to oppression until human endurance gave way before the heavy duties laid on tea. American independence dates from the throwing of tea chests into Boston harbor.

There is a subtle charm in the taste of tea which makes it irresistible and capable of idealization. Western humorists were not slow to mingle the fragrance of their thought with its aroma. It has not the arrogance of wine, the self-consciousness of coffee, nor the simpering innocence of cocoa. Already in 1711, says the *Spectator*: "I would therefore in a particular manner recommend these my speculations to all well-regulated families that set apart an hour every morning for tea, bread and butter; and would earnestly advise them for their good to order this paper to be punctually served up and to be looked upon as a part of the tea-equipage." Samuel Johnson draws his own portrait as "a hardened and shameless tea-drinker, who for twenty years diluted his meals with only the infusion of the fascinating plant; who with tea amused the evening, with tea solaced the midnight, and with tea welcomed the morning."

Charles Lamb, a professed devotee, sounded the true note of teaism when he wrote that the greatest pleasure he knew was to do a good action by stealth, and to have found it out by accident. For teaism is the art of concealing beauty that you may discover it, of suggesting what you dare not reveal. It is the noble secret of laughing at yourself, calmly yet thoroughly, and is thus humor itself—the smile of philosophy. All genuine humorists may in this sense be called tea philosophers—Thackeray, for instance, and, of course, Shakespeare. The poets of the Decadence (when was not the world in decadence?), in their protests against materialism, have, to a certain extent, also opened the way to teaism. Perhaps nowadays it is our demure contemplation of the imperfect that the West and the East can meet in mutual consolation.

The Taoists relate that at the great beginning of the no-beginning, spirit and matter met in mortal combat. At last the Yellow Emperor, the Sun of Heaven, triumphed over Chu Yung, the demon of darkness and earth. The Titan, in his death agony, struck his head against the solar vault and shivered the blue dome of jade into fragments. The stars lost their nests, the moon wandered aimlessly among the wild chasms of the night. In despair the Yellow Emperor sought far and wide for the repairer of the Heavens. He had not to search in vain. Out of the eastern sea rose a queen, the divine Nu Wa, horn-crowned and dragon-tailed, resplendent in her armor of fire. She welded the five-colored rainbow in her magic cauldron and rebuilt the Chinese sky. But it is also told that Nu Wa forgot to fill two tiny crevices in the blue firmament. Thus began the dualism of love—two souls rolling through space and never at rest until they join together to complete the universe. Everyone has to build anew his sky of hope and peace.

The heaven of modern humanity is indeed shattered in the Cyclopean struggle for wealth and power. The world is groping in the shadow of egotism and vulgarity. Knowledge is bought through a bad conscience, benevolence practiced for the sake of utility. The East and West, like two dragons tossed in a sea of ferment, in vain strive to regain the jewel of life. We need a Nu Wa again to repair the grand devastation; we await the great avatar. Meanwhile, let us have a sip of tea. The afternoon glow is brightening the bamboos, the fountains are bubbling with delight, the soughing of the pines is heard in our kettle. Let us dream of evanescence, and linger in the beautiful foolishness of things.

The Schools of Tea

Tea is a work of art and needs a master hand to bring out its noblest qualities. We have good and bad tea, as we have good and bad paintings—generally the latter. There is no single recipe for making the perfect tea, as there are no rules for producing a Titian or a Sesson. Each preparation of the leaves has its individuality, its special affinity with water and heat, its hereditary memories to recall, its own method of telling a story. The truly beautiful must be always in it. How much do we not suffer through the constant failure of society to recognize this simple and fundamental law of art and life; Lichihlai, a Sung poet, has sadly remarked that there were three most deplorable things in the world: the spoiling of fine youths through false education, the degradation of fine paintings through vulgar admiration, and the utter waste of fine tea through incompetent manipulation.

Like art, tea has its periods and its schools. Its evolution may be roughly divided into three main stages: the boiled tea, the whipped tea, and the steeped tea. We moderns belong to the last school. These several methods of appreciating the beverage are indicative of the spirit of the age in which they prevailed. For life is an expression, our unconscious actions the constant betrayal of our innermost thought. Confucius said that "man hideth not." Perhaps we reveal ourselves too much in small things because we have so little of the great to conceal. The tiny incidents of daily routine are as much a commentary of racial ideals as the highest flight of philosophy or poetry. Even as the difference in favorite vintage marks the separate idiosyncrasies of different periods and nationalities of Europe, so the tea ideals characterize the various moods of oriental culture. The cake tea which was boiled, the powdered tea which was whipped, the leaf tea which was steeped, mark the distinct emotional impulses

of the T'ang, the Sung, and the Ming dynasties of China. If we were inclined to borrow the much-abused terminology of art classification, we might designate them respectively, the classic, the romantic, and the naturalistic schools of tea.

The tea plant, a native of southern China, was known from very early times to Chinese botany and medicine. It is alluded to in the classics under the various names of *t'o, sheh, chuan, chia,* and *ming,* and was highly prized for possessing the virtues of relieving fatigue, delighting the soul, strengthening the will, and repairing the eyesight. It was not only administered as an internal dose, but often applied externally in the form of paste to alleviate rheumatic pains. The Taoists claimed it as an important ingredient of the elixir of immortality. The Buddhists used it extensively to prevent drowsiness during their long hours of meditation.

By the fourth and fifth centuries tea became a favorite beverage among the inhabitants of the Yangtse-Kiang valley. It was about this time that the modern ideograph *ch'a* was coined, evidently a corruption of the classic *t'ou.* The poets of the southern dynasties have left some fragments of their fervent adoration of the "froth of the liquid jade." Then emperors used to bestow some rare preparation of the leaves on their high ministers as a reward for eminent services. Yet the method of drinking tea at this stage was primitive in the extreme. The leaves were steamed, crushed in a mortar, made into a cake, and boiled together with rice, ginger, salt, orange peel, spices, milk, and sometimes with onions! The custom obtains at the present day among the Tibetans and various Mongolian tribes, who make a curious syrup of these ingredients. The use of lemon slices by the Russians, who learned to take tea from the Chinese caravansaries, points to the survival of the ancient method.

It needed the genius of the T'ang dynasty to emancipate tea from its crude state and lead to its final idealization. With Lu Wu in the middle of the eighth century we have our first apostle of tea. He was born in an age when Buddhism, Taoism, and Confucianism were seeking mutual synthesis. The pantheistic symbolism of the time was urging one to mirror the universal in the particular. Lu Wu, a poet, saw in the tea service the same harmony and order which reigned through all things. In his celebrated work, the *Ch'a Ching* ("The Holy Scripture of Tea") he formulated the code of tea. He has since been worshipped as the tutelary god of the Chinese tea merchants.

The *Ch'a Ching* consists of three volumes and ten chapters. In the first chapter Lu Wu treats the nature of the tea plant, in the second the implements for gathering the leaves, in the third the selection of the leaves. According to him the best quality leaves must have "creases like the leathern boot of Tartar horsemen, curl like the dewlap of a mighty bullock, unfold like a mist rising out of a ravine, gleam like a lake touched by a zephyr, and be wet and soft like fine earth newly swept by rain."

The fourth chapter is devoted to the enumeration and description of the twenty-four members of the tea equipage, beginning with the tripod brazier and ending with the bamboo cabinet for containing all these utensils. Here we notice Lu Wu's predilection for Taoist symbolism. Also it is interesting to observe in this connection the influence of tea on Chinese ceramics. The celestial porcelain, as is well known, had its origin in an attempt to reproduce the exquisite shade of jade, resulting, in the T'ang dynasty, in the blue glaze of the south, and the white glaze of the north. Lu Wu considered the blue as the ideal color for the teacup, as it lent additional greenness to the beverage, whereas the white made it look pinkish and distasteful. It was because he used cake tea. Later on, when the tea masters of Sung took to the powdered tea, they preferred heavy bowls of blue-black and dark brown. The Mings, with their steeped tea, rejoiced in light ware of white porcelain.

In the fifth chapter Lu Wu describes the method of making tea. He eliminates all ingredients except salt. He dwells also on the much-discussed question of the choice of water and the degree of boiling it. According to him, the mountain spring is the best, the river water and the spring water come next in the order of excellence. There are three stages of boiling: the first boil is when the little bubbles like the eye of fishes swim on the surface; the second boil is when the bubbles are like crystal beads rolling in a fountain; the third boil is when the billows surge wildly in the kettle. The cake tea is roasted before the fire until it becomes soft like a baby's arm and is shredded into powder between pieces of fine paper. Salt is put in the first boil, the tea in the second. At the third boil, a dipperful of cold water is poured into the kettle to settle the tea and revive the "youth of the water." Then the beverage was poured into cups and drunk. O nectar! The filmy leaflet hung like scaly clouds in a serene sky or floated like waterlilies on emerald streams. It was of such a beverage that Lu T'ung, a T'ang poet, wrote: "The first cup moistens my lips and throat, the second cup breaks my loneliness, the third cup searches my barren entrail but to find therein some five thousand volumes of odd ideographs. The fourth cup raises a slight perspiration—all the wrong of life passes away through my pores. At the fifth cup I am purified; the sixth cup calls me to the realms of immortals. The seventh cup—ah, but I could take no more! I only feel the breath of cool wind that rises in my sleeves. Where is Horaisan? Let me ride on this sweet breeze and waft away thither."

The remaining chapters of the *Ch'a Ching* treat of the vulgarity of the ordinary methods of tea drinking, a historical summary of illustrious tea drinkers, the famous tea plantations of China, the possible variations of the tea service and illustrations of the tea utensils. The last is unfortunately lost.

The appearance of the *Ch'a Ching* must have created considerable sensation at the time. Lu Wu was befriended by the Emperor T'ai Tsung (763–779),

and his fame attracted many followers. Some ex-
quisites were said to have been able to detect the tea
made by Lu Wu from that of his disciples. One
mandarin has his name immortalized by his failure
to appreciate the tea of this great master.

In the Sung dynasty the whipped tea came into
fashion and created the second school of tea. The
leaves were ground to fine powder in a small stone
mill, and the preparation was whipped in hot water
by a delicate whisk made of split bamboo. The new
process led to some change in the tea equipage of
Lu Wu, as well as the choice of leaves. Salt was dis-
carded forever. The enthusiasm of the Sung people
for tea knew no bounds. Epicures vied with each
other in discovering new varieties, and regular tour-
naments were held to decide their superiority. The
Emperor Huei Tsung (1101–1124), who was too
great an artist to be a well-behaved monarch, lav-
ished his treasures on the attainment of rare species.
He himself wrote a dissertation on the twenty kinds
of tea, among which he prizes the "white tea" as of
the rarest and finest quality.

The tea ideal of the Sungs differed from the
T'angs even as their notion of life differed. They
sought to actualize what their predecessors tried to

symbolize. To the neo-Confucian mind the cosmic law was not reflected in the phenomenal world, but the phenomenal world was the cosmic law itself. Eons were but moments—nirvana always within grasp. The Taoist conception that immortality lay in the eternal change permeated all their modes of thought. It was the process, not the deed, which was interesting. It was the completing, not the completion, which was really vital. Man came thus at once face to face with nature. A new meaning grew into the art of life. The tea began to be not a poetical pastime, but one of the methods of self-realization. Wang Yuan Chih eulogized tea as "flooding his soul like a direct appeal, that its delicate bitterness reminded him of the after-taste of a good counsel." Sotumpa wrote of the strength of the immaculate purity in tea which defied corruption as a truly virtuous man. Among the Buddhists, the southern Zen sect, which incorporated so much of Taoist doctrines, formulated an elaborate ritual of tea. The monks gathered before the image of Bodhidharma and drank tea out of a single bowl with the profound formality of a holy sacrament. It was this Zen ritual which finally developed into the tea ceremony of Japan in the fifteenth century.

Unfortunately the sudden outburst of the Mongol tribes in the thirteenth century, which resulted in the devastation and conquest of China under the barbaric rule of the Yuen emperors, destroyed all the fruits of Sung culture. The native dynasty of the Mings which attempted re-nationalization in the middle of the fifteenth century was harassed by internal troubles, and China again fell under the alien rule of the Manchus in the seventeenth century. Manners and customs changed to leave no vestige of the former times. The powdered tea is entirely forgotten. We find a Ming commentator at loss to recall the shape of the tea whisk mentioned in one of the Sung classics. Tea is now taken by steeping the leaves in hot water in a bowl or cup. The reason why the western world is innocent of the older method of drinking tea is explained by the fact that Europe knew it only at the close of the Ming dynasty.

To the latter-day Chinese tea is a delicious beverage, but not an ideal. The long woes of his country have robbed him of the zest for the meaning of life. He has become modern, that is to say, old and disenchanted. He has lost that sublime faith in illusions which constitutes the eternal youth and vigor of the poets and ancients. He is an eclectic and politely accepts the traditions of the universe. He toys with nature, but does not condescend to conquer or worship her. His leaf tea is often wonderful with its flower-like aroma, but the romance of the T'ang and Sung ceremonials are not to be found in his cup.

Japan, which followed closely on the footsteps of Chinese civilization, has known the tea in all its three stages. As early as the year 729 we read of the Emperor Shomu giving tea to one hundred monks at his palace in Nara. The leaves were probably imported by our ambassadors to the T'ang court and prepared in the way then in fashion. In 801 the monk Saicho brought back some seeds and planted them in Yeisan. Many tea gardens are heard of in the succeeding centuries, as well as the delight of the aristocracy and priesthood in the beverage. The Sung tea reached us in 1191 with the return of Yeisai-zenji, who went there to study the southern Zen school. The new seeds which he carried home were successfully planted in three places, one of which, the Uji district near Kyoto, bears still the name of producing the best tea in the world. The southern Zen spread with marvellous rapidity, and with it the

tea ritual and the tea ideal of the Sung. By the fifteenth century, under the patronage of the Shogun,
Ashikaga-Voshinasa, the tea ceremony is fully con-
stituted and made into an independent and secular
performance. Since then teaism is fully established
in Japan. The use of the steeped tea of the later
China is comparatively recent among us, being only
known since the middle of the seventeenth century.
It has replaced the powdered tea in ordinary consumption, though the latter still continues to hold
its place as the tea of teas.

It is in the Japanese tea ceremony that we see the
culmination of tea ideals. Our successful resistance
of the Mongol invasion in 1281 had enabled us to
carry on the Sung movement so disastrously cut off
in China itself through the nomadic inroad. Tea
with us became more than an idealization of the
form of drinking; it is a religion of the art of life.
The beverage grew to be an excuse for the worship
of purity and refinement, a sacred function at which
the host and guest joined to produce for that occasion the utmost beatitude of the mundane. The tearoom was an oasis in the dreary waste of existence
where weary travellers could meet to drink from the
common spring of art-appreciation. The ceremony

was an improvised drama whose plot was woven about the tea, the flowers, and the paintings. Not a color to disturb the tone of the room, not a sound to mar the rhythm of things, not a gesture to obtrude on the harmony, not a word to break the unity of the surroundings, all movements to be performed simply and naturally—such were the aims of the tea ceremony. And strangely enough it was often successful. A subtle philosophy lay behind it all. Teaism was Taoism in disguise.

Taoism and Zennism

The connection of Zennism with tea is proverbial. We have already remarked that the tea ceremony was a development of the Zen ritual. The name of Lao-tzu, the founder of Taoism, is also intimately associated with the history of tea. It is written in the Chinese school manual concerning the origin of habits and customs that the ceremony of offering tea to a guest began with Kwanyin, a well-known disciple of Lao-tzu, who first at the gate of the Han Pass presented to the "Old Philosopher" a cup of the golden elixir. We shall not stop to discuss the authenticity of such tales, which are valuable, however, as confirming the early use of the beverage by the Taoists. Our interest in Taoism and Zennism here lies mainly in those ideas regarding life and art which are so embodied in what we call teaism.

It is to be regretted that as yet there appears to be no adequate presentation of the Taoists and Zen doctrines in any foreign language, though we have had several laudable attempts.

Translation is always a treason, and as a Ming author observes, can at its best be only the reverse side of a brocade—all the threads are there, but not the subtlety of color or design. But, after all, what great doctrine is there which is easy to expound? The ancient sages never put their teachings in systematic form. They spoke in paradoxes, for they were afraid of uttering half-truths. They began by talking like fools and ended by making their hearers wise. Lao-tzu himself, with his quaint humor, says, "If people of inferior intelligence hear of the Tao, they laugh immensely. It would not be the Tao unless they laughed at it."

The Tao literally means a Path. It has been severally translated as the Way, the Absolute, the Law, Nature, Supreme Reason, the Mode. These renderings are not incorrect, for the use of the term by the

Taoists differs according to the subject matter of the inquiry. Lao-tzu himself spoke of it thus: "There is a thing which is all-containing, which was born before the existence of Heaven and Earth. How silent! How solitary! It stands alone and changes not. It revolves without danger to itself and is the mother of the universe. I do not know its name and so call it the path. With reluctance I call it the infinite. Infinity is the fleeting, the fleeting is the vanishing, the vanishing is the reverting." The Tao is in the passage rather than the path. It is the spirit of cosmic change—the eternal growth which returns upon itself to produce new forms. It recoils upon itself like the dragon, the beloved symbol of the Taoists. It folds and unfolds as do the clouds. The Tao might be spoken of as the great transition. Subjectively it is the mood of the universe. Its absolute is the relative.

It should be remembered in the first place that Taoism, like its legitimate successor Zennism, represents the individualistic trend of the southern Chinese mind in contradistinction to the communism of northern China which expressed itself in Confucianism. The Middle Kingdom is as vast as Europe and has a differentiation of idiosyncrasies marked by the two great river systems which traverse it. The Yangtse-Kiang and Hoang-Ho are respectively the Mediterranean and the Baltic. Even today, in spite of centuries of unification, the Southern Celestial differs in his thoughts and beliefs from his northern brother as a member of the Latin race differs from the Teuton. In ancient days, when communication was even more difficult than at present, and especially during the feudal period, this difference in thought was most pronounced. The art and poetry of the one breathes an atmosphere entirely distinct from that of the other. In Lao-tzu and his followers and in Kutsugen, the forerunner of the Yangtse-Kiang nature poets, we find an idealism quite inconsistent with the prosaic ethical notions of their contemporary northern writers. Lao-tzu lived five centuries before the Christian Era.

The germ of Taoist speculation may be found long before the advent of Lao-tzu, surnamed the Long-Eared. The archaic records of China, especially the *Book of Changes*, foreshadow his thought. But the great respect paid to the laws and customs of that classic period of Chinese civilization which culminated with the establishment of the Chou dynasty in the sixteenth century B.C., kept the development of individualism in check for a long while, so that it was not until after the disintegration of the Chou dynasty and the establishment of innumerable independent kingdoms that it was able to blossom forth in the luxuriance of free thought. Lao-tzu and Soshi (Chuang-tzu) were both Southerners and the greatest exponents of the New School. On the other hand Confucius with his numerous disciples aimed at retaining ancestral conventions. Taoism cannot be understood without some knowledge of Confucianism and vice versa.

We have said that the Taoist absolute was the relative. In ethics the Taoist railed at the laws and the moral codes of society, for to them right and wrong were but relative terms. Definition is always limitation—the "fixed" and "unchangeless" are but terms expressive of a stoppage of growth. Said Kuzugen, "The Sages move the world." Our standards of morality are begotten of the past needs of society, but is society to remain always the same? The observance of communal traditions involves a constant sacrifice of the individual to the state. Education, in order to keep up the mighty delusion, encourages a species of ignorance. People are not

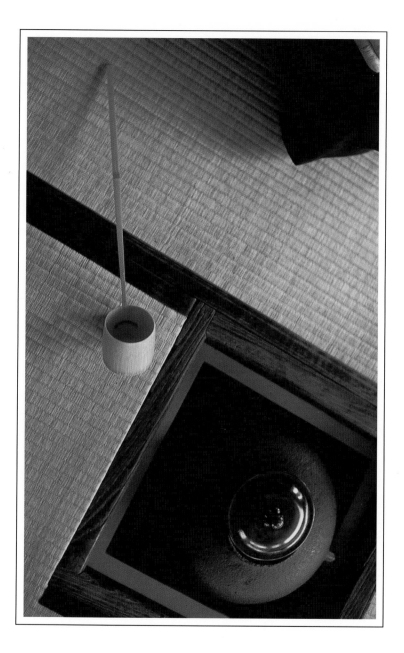

taught to be really virtuous, but to behave properly. We are wicked because we are frightfully self-conscious. We never forgive others because we know that we ourselves are in the wrong. We nurse a conscience because we are afraid to tell the truth to others; we take refuge in pride because we are afraid to tell the truth to ourselves. How can one be serious with the world when the world itself is so ridiculous! The spirit of barter is everywhere. Honor and chastity! Behold the complacent salesman retailing the good and true. One can even buy a so-called religion, which is really but common morality sanctified with flowers and music. Rob the church of her accessories and what remains behind? Yet the trusts thrive marvellously, for the prices are absurdly cheap—a prayer for a ticket to heaven, a diploma for an honorable citizenship. Hide yourself under a bushel quickly, for if your real usefulness were known to the world you would soon be knocked down to the highest bidder by the public auctioneer. Why do men and women like to advertise themselves so much? Is it not but an instinct derived from the days of slavery?

The virility of the idea lies not less in its power of breaking through contemporary thought than in its capacity for dominating subsequent movements. Taoism was an active power during the Shin dynasty, that epoch of Chinese unification from which we derive the name *China*. It would be interesting had we time to note its influence on contemporary thinkers, the mathematicians, writers on law and war, the mystics and alchemists and the later nature poets of the Yangtse-Kiang. We should not even ignore those speculators on reality who doubted whether a white horse was real because he was white, or because he was solid, nor the conversationalists of the Six dynasties who, like the Zen philosophers, revelled in discussions concerning the pure and the abstract. Above all we should pay homage to Taoism for what it has done toward the formation of the celestial character, giving to it a certain capacity for reserve and refinement as "warm as jade." Chinese history is full of instances in which the votaries of Taoism, princes and hermits alike, followed with varied and interesting results the teachings of their creed. The tale will not be without its quota of instruction and amusement. It will be rich in anecdotes, allegories, and aphorisms. We would fain be on speaking terms with the delightful emperor who never died because he never lived. We may ride the

wind with Lieh-tzu and find it absolutely quiet because we ourselves are the wind, or dwell in mid-air
with the Aged One of the Hoang-Ho, who lived
between heaven and earth because he was subject
to neither the one nor the other. Even in that
grotesque apology for Taoism which we find in
China at the present day, we can revel in a wealth of
imagery impossible to find in any other cult.

But the chief contribution of Taoism to Asiatic
life has been in the realm of aesthetics. Chinese his-
torians have always spoken of Taoism as the "art of
being in the world," for it deals with the present—
ourselves. It is in us that God meets with nature,
and yesterday parts from tomorrow. The present is
the moving infinity, the legitimate sphere of the relative. Relativity seeks adjustment; adjustment is art.
The art of life lies in a constant readjustment to our
surroundings. Taoism accepts the mundane as it is
and, unlike the Confucians and the Buddhists, tries
to find beauty in our world of woe and worry. The
Sung allegory of the Three Vinegar Tasters explains
admirably the trend of the three doctrines. Shakyamuni, Confucius, and Lao-tzu once stood before a
jar of vinegar—the emblem of life—and each
dipped in his finger to taste the brew. The matter-

of-fact Confucius found it sour, the Buddha called it bitter, and Lao-tzu pronounced it sweet.

The Taoists claimed that the comedy of life could be made more interesting if everyone would preserve the unities. To keep the proportion of things and give place to others without losing one's own position was the secret of success in the mundane drama. We must know the whole play in order to properly act our parts; the conception of totality must never be lost in that of the individual. This Lao-tzu illustrates by his favorite metaphor of the vacuum. He claimed that only in vacuum lay the truly essential. The reality of a room, for instance, was to be found in the vacant space enclosed by the roof and walls, not in the roof and walls themselves. The usefulness of a water pitcher dwelt in the emptiness where water might be put, not in the form of the pitcher or the material of which it was made. Vacuum is all potent because it is all containing. In vacuum alone motion becomes possible. One who could make of himself a vacuum into which others might freely enter would become master of all situations. The whole can always dominate the part.

These Taoists' ideas have greatly influenced all our theories of action, even to those of fencing and wrestling. Jiu-jitsu, the Japanese art of self-defense, owes its name to a passage in the *Tao-te Ching*. In jiu-jitsu one seeks to draw out and exhaust the enemy's strength by non-resistance, vacuum, while conserving one's own strength for victory in the final struggle. In art the importance of the same principle is illustrated by the value of suggestion. In leaving something unsaid the beholder is given a chance to complete the idea and thus a great masterpiece irresistibly rivets your attention until you seem to become actually a part of it. A vacuum is there for you to enter and fill up to the full measure of your aesthetic emotion.

He who had made himself master of the art of living was the Real Man of the Taoist. At birth he enters the realm of dreams only to awaken to reality at death. He tempers his own brightness in order to merge himself into the obscurity of others. He is "reluctant, as one who crosses a stream in winter; hesitating as one who fears the neighborhood; respectful, like a guest; trembling, like ice that is about to melt; unassuming, like a piece of wood not yet carved; vacant, like a valley; formless, like troubled waters." To him the three jewels of life were pity, economy, and modesty.

If now we turn our attention to Zennism we shall find that it emphasizes the teachings of Taoism. *Zen* is a name derived from the Sanskrit word *dhyana*, which signifies meditation. It claims that through consecrated meditation may be attained supreme self-realization. Meditation is one of the six ways through which Buddhahood may be reached, and the Zen sectarians affirm that Shakyamuni laid special stress on this method in his later teachings, handing down the rules to his chief disciple Kashyapa. According to their tradition Kashyapa, the first Zen patriarch, imparted the secret to Ananda, who in turn passed it on to successive patriarchs until it reached Bodhidharma, the twenty-eighth. Bodhidharma came to northern China in the early half of the sixth century and was the first patriarch of Chinese Zen. There is much uncertainty about the history of these patriarchs and their doctrines. In its philosophical aspect early Zennism seems to have affinity on one hand to the Indian Negativism of Nagarjuna and on the other to the Jnana philosophy formulated by Sankaracharya. The first teaching of Zen as we know it at the present day must be attributed to the sixth Chinese patriarch Eno (637–713), founder of

Southern Zen, so-called from the fact of its pre-dominance in southern China. He is closely followed by the great Baso (died 788) who made of Zen a living influence in celestial life. H'akujō (719–814), the pupil of Baso, first instituted the Zen monastery and established a ritual and regulations for its government. In the discussions of the Zen school after the time of Baso we find the play of the Yangtse-Kiang mind causing an accession of native modes of thought in contrast to the former Indian idealism. Whatever sectarian pride may assert to the contrary one cannot help being impressed by the similarity of Southern Zen to the teachings of Lao-tzu and the Taoist conversationalists. In the *Tao-te Ching* we already find allusions to the importance of self-concentration and the need of properly regulating the breath—essential points in the practice of Zen meditation. Some of the best commentaries on the book of Lao-tzu have been written by Zen scholars.

Zennism, like Taoism, is the worship of relativity. One master defines Zen as the art of feeling the polar star in the southern sky. Truth can be reached only through the comprehension of opposites. Again, Zennism, like Taoism, is a strong advocate of

39

individualism. Nothing is real except that which concerns the working of our own minds. Eno, the sixth patriarch, once saw two monks watching the flag of a pagoda fluttering in the wind. One said "It is the wind that moves," the other said "It is the flag that moves"; but Eno explained to them that the real movement was neither of the wind nor the flag, but of something within their own minds. H'akujō was walking in the forest with a disciple when a hare scurried off at their approach. "Why does the hare fly from you?" asked H'akujō. "Because he is afraid of me," was the answer. "No," said the master, "it is because you have a murderous instinct." This dialogue recalls that of Soshi [Chuang-tzu], the Taoist. One day Soshi was walking on the bank of a river with a friend. "How delightfully the fishes are enjoying themselves in the water!" exclaimed Soshi. His friend spake to him thus: "You are not a fish; how do you know that the fishes are enjoying themselves?" "You are not myself," returned Soshi; "how do you know that I do not know that the fishes are enjoying themselves?"

Zen was often opposed to the precepts of orthodox Buddhism even as Taoism was opposed to Confucianism. To the transcendental insight of the

Zen, words were but an encumbrance to thought; the whole sway of Buddhist scriptures only commentaries on personal speculation. The followers of Zen aimed at direct communion with the inner nature of things, regarding their outward accessories only as impediments to a clear perception of truth. It was this love of the abstract that led the Zen to prefer black and white sketches to the elaborately colored paintings of the classic Buddhist School. Some of the Zen even became iconoclastic as a result of their endeavor to recognize the Buddha in themselves rather than through images and symbolism. We find Tankawosho breaking up a wooden statue of Buddha on a wintry day to make a fire. "What sacrilege!" said the horror-stricken bystander. "I wish to get the Shali [precious jewels] out of the ashes," calmly rejoined the Zen. "But you certainly will not get Shali from this image!" was the angry retort, to which Tanka replied, "If I do not, this is certainly not a Buddha and I am committing no sacrilege." Then he turned to warm himself over the kindling fire.

A special contribution of Zen to Eastern thought was its recognition of the mundane as of equal importance with the spiritual. It held that in the great relation of things there was no distinction of small and great, an atom possessing equal possibilities with the universe. The seeker for perfection must discover in his own life the reflection of the inner light. The organization of the Zen monastery was very significant of this point of view. To every member, except the abbot, was assigned some special work in the caretaking of the monastery, and curiously enough, to the novices were committed the lighter duties, while to the most respected and advanced monks were given the more irksome and menial tasks. Such services formed a part of the Zen discipline and every least action must be done absolutely perfectly. Thus many a weighty discussion ensued while weeding the garden, paring a turnip, or serving tea. The whole ideal of teaism is a result of this Zen conception of greatness in the smallest incidents of life. Taoism furnished the basis for aesthetic ideals, Zennism made them practical.

The Tearoom

To European architects brought up on the traditions of stone and brick construction, our Japanese method of building with wood and bamboo seems scarcely worthy to be ranked as architecture. It is but quite recently that a competent student of western architecture has recognized and paid tribute to the remarkable perfection of our great temples. Such being the case as regards our classic architecture, we could hardly expect the outsider to appreciate the subtle beauty of the tearoom, its principles of construction and decoration being entirely different from those of the West.

The tearoom (the *sukiya*) does not pretend to be other than a mere cottage—a straw hut, as we call it. The original ideographs for *sukiya* mean the Abode of Fancy. Latterly the various tea masters substituted various Chinese characters according to their conception of the tearoom, and the term *sukiya* may signify the Abode of Vacancy or the Abode of the Unsymmetrical. It is an abode of fancy inasmuch as it is an ephemeral structure built to house a poetic impulse. It is an abode of vacancy inasmuch as it is devoid of ornamentation except for what may be placed in it to satisfy some aesthetic need of the moment. It is an abode of the unsymmetrical inasmuch as it is consecrated to the worship of the imperfect, purposely leaving something unfinished for the play of the imagination to complete. The ideals of teaism have since the sixteenth century influenced our architecture to such degree that the ordinary Japanese interior of the present day, on account of the extreme simplicity and chasteness of its scheme of decoration, appears to foreigners almost barren.

The first independent tearoom was the creation of Senno-Soyeki, commonly known by his later name of Rikiu, the greatest of all tea masters, who, in the sixteenth century, under the patronage of

Taiko-Hideyoshi, instituted and brought to a high state of perfection the formalities of the tea ceremony. The proportions of the tearoom had been previously determined by Jowo—a famous tea master of the fifteenth century. The early tearoom consisted merely of a portion of the ordinary drawing room partitioned off by screens for the purpose of the tea gathering. The portion partitioned off was called the *kakoi* (enclosure), a name still applied to those tearooms which are built into a house and are not independent constructions. The *sukiya* consists of the tearoom proper, designed to accommodate not more than five persons, a number suggestive of the saying "more than the Graces and less than the Muses," an anteroom (*midsuya*) where the tea utensils are washed and arranged before being brought in, a portico (*machiai*) in which the guests wait until they receive the summons to enter the tearoom, and a garden path (the *roji*) which connects the *machiai* with the tearoom. The tearoom is unimpressive in appearance. It is smaller than the smallest of Japanese houses, while the materials used in its construction are intended to give the suggestion of refined poverty. Yet we must remember that all this is the result of profound artistic forethought, and that the details have been worked out with care perhaps even greater than that expended on the building of the richest palaces and temples. A good tearoom is more costly than an ordinary mansion, for the selection of its materials, as well as its workmanship, requires immense care and precision. Indeed, the carpenters employed by the tea masters form a distinct and highly honored class among artisans, their work being no less delicate than that of the makers of lacquer cabinets.

The tearoom is not only different from any production of western architecture, but also contrasts strongly with the classical architecture of Japan itself. Our ancient noble edifices, whether secular or ecclesiastical, were not to be despised even as regards their mere size. The few that have been spared in the disastrous conflagrations of centuries are still capable of awing us by the grandeur and richness of their decoration. Huge pillars of wood from two to three feet in diameter and from thirty to forty feet high, supported, by a complicated network of brackets, the enormous beams which groaned under the weight of the tile-covered slanting roofs. The material and mode of construction, though weak against fire, proved itself strong against earthquakes, and was well suited to the climatic conditions of the country. In the Golden Hall of Horiuji and the Pagoda of Yakushiji, we have noteworthy examples of the durability of our wooden architecture. These buildings have practically stood intact for nearly twelve centuries. The interior of the old temples and palaces was profusely decorated. In the Hoodo temple at Uji, dating from the tenth century, we can still see the elaborate canopy and gilded baldachinos, many-colored and inlaid with mirrors and mother-of-pearl, as well as remains of the paintings and sculpture which formerly covered the walls. Later, at Nikko and in the Nijo castle in Kyoto, we see structural beauty sacrificed to a wealth of ornamentation which in color and exquisite detail equals the utmost gorgeousness of Arabian or Moorish effort.

The simplicity and purism of the tearoom resulted from emulation of the Zen monastery. A Zen monastery differs from those of other Buddhist sects inasmuch as it is meant only to be a dwelling place for the monks. Its chapel is not a place of worship or pilgrimage, but a college room where the students congregate for discussion and the practice of meditation. The room is bare except for a central alcove in which, behind the altar, is a statue of Bod-

hidharma, the founder of the sect, or of Shakyamuni attended by Kashyapa and Ananda, the two
earliest Zen patriarchs. On the altar, flowers and incense are offered up in memory of the great contributions which these sages made to Zen. We have
already said that it was the ritual instituted by the
Zen monks of successively drinking tea out of a
bowl before the image of Bodhidharma, which laid
the foundations of the tea ceremony. We might add
here that the altar of the Zen chapel was the proto-
type of the *tokonoma*—the place of honor in a Japanese room where paintings and flowers are placed for
the edification of the guests.

All our great tea masters were students of Zen
and attempted to introduce the spirit of Zennism
into the actualities of life. Thus the room, like the
other equipment of the tea ceremony, reflects many
of the Zen doctrines. The size of the orthodox tearoom, which is four mats and a half, or ten feet
square, is determined by a passage in the sutra of
Vikramaditya. In that interesting work, Vikramaditya welcomes the Saint Manjushri and eighty-four
thousand disciples of Buddha in a room of this
size—an allegory based on the theory of the non-
existence of space to the truly enlightened. Again

the *roji,* the garden path which leads from the *machiai* to the tearoom, signified the first stage of meditation—the passage into self-illumination. The *roji* was intended to break connection with the outside world, and to produce a fresh sensation conducive to the full enjoyment of aestheticism in the tearoom itself. One who has trodden this garden path cannot fail to remember how his spirit, as he walked in the twilight of evergreens over the regular irregularities of the stepping stones, beneath which lay dried pine needles, and passed beside the moss-covered granite lanterns, became uplifted above ordinary thoughts. One may be in the midst of a city, and yet feel as if he were in the forest far away from the dust and din of civilization. Great was the ingenuity displayed by the tea masters in producing these effects of serenity and purity. The nature of the sensations to be aroused in passing through the *roji* differed with different tea masters. Some, like Rikiu, aimed at utter loneliness, and claimed the secret of making a *roji* was contained in the ancient ditty:

> I look beyond;
> Flowers are not,
> Nor tinted leaves.

On the sea beach
A solitary cottage stands
In the waning light
Of an autumn eve.

Others, like Kobori-Enshiu, sought for a different effect. Enshiu said the idea of the garden path was to be found in the following verse:

A cluster of summer trees,
A bit of the sea,
A pale evening moon.

It is not difficult to gather his meaning. He wished to create the attitude of a newly awakened soul still lingering amid shadowy dreams of the past, yet bathing in the sweet unconsciousness of a mellow spiritual light, and yearning for the freedom that lay in the expanse beyond.

Thus prepared the guest will silently approach the sanctuary, and, if a samurai, will leave his sword on the rack beneath the eaves, the tearoom being preeminently the house of peace. Then he will bend low and creep into the room through a small door not more than three feet in height. This proceeding was incumbent on all guests—high and low alike—and was intended to inculcate humility. The order of precedence having been mutually agreed upon while resting in the *machiai,* the guests one by one will enter noiselessly and take their seats, first making obeisance to the picture or flower arrangement on the *tokonoma.* The host will not enter the room until all the guests have seated themselves and quiet reigns with nothing to break the silence save the note of the boiling water in the iron kettle. The kettle sings well, for pieces of iron are so arranged in the bottom as to produce a peculiar melody in which one may hear the echoes of a cataract muffled by clouds, of a distant sea breaking among the rocks, a rainstorm sweeping through a bamboo forest, or of the soughing of pines on some faraway hill.

Even in the daytime the light in the room is subdued, for the low eaves of the slanting roof admit but few of the sun's rays. Everything is sober in tint from the ceiling to the floor; the guests themselves have carefully chosen garments of unobtrusive colors. The mellowness of age is over all, everything suggestive of recent acquirement being tabooed save only the one note of contrast furnished by the bamboo dipper and the linen napkin, both immaculately white and new. However faded the tearoom and the tea equipage may seem, everything is absolutely clean. Not a particle of dust will be found in the darkest corner, for if any exists the host is not a tea master. One of the first requisites of a tea master is the knowledge of how to sweep, clean, and wash, for there is an art in cleaning and dusting. A piece of antique metal work must not be attacked with the unscrupulous zeal of the Dutch housewife. Dripping water from a flower vase need not be wiped away, for it may be suggestive of dew and coolness.

In this connection there is a story of Rikiu which well illustrates the ideas of cleanliness entertained by the tea masters. Rikiu was watching his son Shoan as he swept and watered the garden path. "Not clean enough," said Rikiu, when Shoan had finished his task, and bade him try again. After a weary hour the son turned to Rikiu: "Father, there is nothing more to be done. The steps have been washed for the third time, the stone lanterns and the trees are well sprinkled with water, moss and lichens are shining with a fresh verdure; not a twig, not a leaf have I left on the ground." "Young fool," chided the tea master, "that is not the way a garden path should be swept." Saying this, Rikiu stepped into the garden, shook a tree and scattered over the garden gold and crimson leaves, scraps of the brocade of autumn! What Rikiu demanded was not cleanliness alone, but the beautiful and the natural also.

The name, *Abode of Fancy*, implies a structure created to meet some individual artistic requirement. The tearoom is made for the tea master, not the tea master for the tearoom. It is not intended for posterity and is therefore ephemeral. The idea that everyone should have a house of his own is based on an ancient custom of the Japanese race, Shinto superstition ordaining that every dwelling should be evacuated on the death of its chief occupant. Perhaps there may have been some unrealized sanitary reason for this practice. Another early custom was that a newly built house should be provided for each couple that married. It is on account of such customs that we find the Imperial capitals so frequently removed from one site to another in ancient days. The rebuilding, every twenty years, of Ise Temple, the supreme shrine of the Sun Goddess, is an example of one of these ancient rites which still obtain at the present day. The observance of these customs was only possible with some such form of construction as that furnished by our system of wooden architecture, easily pulled down, easily built up. A more lasting style, employing brick and stone, would have rendered migrations impracticable, as indeed they became when the more stable and massive wooden construction of China was adopted by us after the Nara period.

With the predominance of Zen individualism in the fifteenth century, however, the old idea became imbued with a deeper significance as conceived in connection with the tearoom. Zennism, with the Buddhist theory of evanescence and its demands for the mastery of spirit over matter, recognized the house only as a temporary refuge for the body. The body itself was but as a hut in the wilderness, a flimsy shelter made by tying together the grasses that grew around—when these ceased to be bound together they again became resolved into the original waste. In the tearoom fugitiveness is suggested in the thatched roof, frailty in the slender pillars, lightness in the bamboo support, apparent carelessness in the use of commonplace materials. The eternal is to be found only in the spirit which, embodied in these simple surroundings, beautifies them with the subtle light of its refinement.

That the tearoom should be built to suit some individual taste is an enforcement of the principle of
vitality in art. Art, to be fully appreciated, must be
true to contemporaneous life. It is not that we should
ignore the claims of posterity, but that we should
seek to enjoy the present more. It is not that we
should disregard the creations of the past, but that we
should try to assimilate them into our consciousness.
Slavish conformity to traditions and formulas fetters
the expression of individuality in architecture. We can
but weep over those senseless imitations of European
buildings which one beholds in modern Japan. We
marvel why, among the most progressive western nations, architecture should be so devoid of originality,
so replete with repetitions of obsolete styles. Perhaps
we are now passing through an age of democratiza-
tion in art, while awaiting the rise of some princely
master who shall establish a new dynasty. Would that
we loved the ancients more and copied them less! It
has been said that the Greeks were great because they
never drew from the antique.

The term, *Abode of Vacancy*, besides conveying the
Taoist theory of the all-containing, involves the conception of a continued need of change in decorative
motives. The tearoom is absolutely empty, except for

 55

what may be placed there temporarily to satisfy some aesthetic mood. Some special art object is brought in for the occasion, and everything else is selected and arranged to enhance the beauty of the principal theme. One cannot listen to different pieces of music at the same time, a real comprehension of the beautiful being possible only through concentration upon some central motive. Thus it will be seen that the system of decoration in our tearooms is opposed to that which obtains in the West, where the interior of a house is often converted into a museum. To a Japanese, accustomed to simplicity of ornamentation and frequent change of decorative method, a western interior permanently filled with a vast array of pictures, statuary, and bric-à-brac gives the impression of mere vulgar display of riches. It calls for a mighty wealth of appreciation to enjoy the constant sight of even a masterpiece, and limitless indeed must be the capacity for artistic feeling in those who can exist day after day in the midst of such confusion of color and form as is to be often seen in the homes of Europe and America.

The *Abode of the Unsymmetrical* suggests another phase of our decorative scheme. The absence of symmetry in Japanese art objects has been often com-

mented on by western critics. This, also, is a result
of a working out through Zennism of Taoist ideals.
Confucianism, with its deep-seated idea of dualism,
and Northern Buddhism with its worship of a trin-
ity, were in no way opposed to the expression of
symmetry. As a matter of fact, if we study the ancient bronzes of China or the religious arts of the
T'ang dynasty and the Nara period, we shall recognize a constant striving after symmetry. The decoration of our classical interiors was decidedly regular
in its arrangement. The Taoist and Zen conception
of perfection, however, was different. The dynamic
nature of their philosophy laid more stress upon the
process through which perfection was sought than
upon perfection itself. True beauty could be discov-
ered only by one who mentally completed the in-
complete. The virility of life and art lay in its
possibilities for growth. In the tearoom it is left for
each guest in imagination to complete the total effect in relation to himself. Since Zennism has become the prevailing mode of thought, the art of the
extreme Orient has purposely avoided the symmet-
rical as expressing not only completion, but repetition. Uniformity of design was considered as fatal
to the freshness of imagination. Thus, landscapes,

birds, and flowers became the favorite subjects for depiction rather than the human figure, the latter being present in the person of the beholder himself. We are often too much in evidence as it is, and in spite of our vanity even self-regard is apt to become monotonous.

In the tearoom the fear of repetition is a constant presence. The various objects for the decoration of a room should be so selected that no color or design shall be repeated. If you have a living flower, a painting of flowers is not allowable. If you are using a round kettle, the water pitcher should be angular. A cup with a black glaze should not be associated with a tea-caddy of black lacquer. In placing a vase or an incense burner on the *tokonoma,* care should be taken not to put it in the exact center, lest it divide the space into equal halves. The pillar of the *tokonoma* should be of a different kind of wood from the other pillars, in order to break any suggestion of monotony in the room.

Here again the Japanese method of interior decoration differs from that of the Occident, where we see objects arrayed symmetrically on mantlepieces and elsewhere. In western houses we are often confronted with what appears to us useless reiteration. We find it trying to talk to a man while his full-length portrait stares at us from behind his back. We wonder which is real, he of the picture or he who talks, and feel a curious conviction that one of them must be fraud. Many a time have we sat at a festive board contemplating, with a secret shock to our digestion, the representation of abundance on the dining-room walls. Why these pictured victims of chase and sport, the elaborate carvings of fishes and fruit? Why the display of family plates, reminding us of those who have dined and are dead?

The simplicity of the tearoom and its freedom from vulgarity make it truly a sanctuary from the vexations of the outer world. There and there alone can one consecrate himself to undisturbed adoration of the beautiful. In the sixteenth century the tearoom afforded a welcome respite from labor to the fierce warriors and statesmen engaged in the unification and reconstruction of Japan. In the seventeenth century, after the strict formalism of the Tokugawa rule had been developed, it offered the only opportunity possible for the free communion of artistic spirits. Before a great work of art there was no distinction between *daimyo*, samurai, and commoner. Nowadays industrialism is making true refinement more and more difficult all the world over. Do we not need the tearoom more than ever?

Art Appreciation

Have you heard the Taoist tale of "The Taming of the Harp?"

Once in the hoary ages in the Ravine of Lung Men stood a *kiri* tree, a veritable king of the forest. It reared its head to talk to the stars; its roots struck deep into the earth, mingling their bronzed coils with those of the silver dragon that slept beneath. And it came to pass that a mighty wizard made of this tree a wondrous harp, whose stubborn spirit should be tamed but by the greatest of musicians. For long the instrument was treasured by the Emperor of China, but all in vain were the efforts of those who in turn tried to draw melody from its strings. In response to their utmost strivings there came from the harp but harsh notes of disdain, ill-according with the songs they fain would sing. The harp refused to recognize a master.

At last came Pai Ya, the prince of harpists. With tender hand he caressed the harp as one might seek to soothe an unruly horse, and softly touched the chords. He sang of nature and the seasons, of high mountains and flowing waters, and all the memories of the tree awoke! Once more the sweet breath of spring played amidst its branches. The young cataracts, as they danced down the ravine, laughed to the budding flowers. Anon were heard the dreamy voices of summer with its myriad insects, the gentle pattering of rain, the wail of the cuckoo. Hark! a tiger roars—the valley answers again. It is autumn; in the desert night, sharp like a sword gleams the moon upon the frosted grass. Now winter reigns, and through the snow-filled air swirl flocks of swans and rattling hailstones beat upon the boughs with fierce delight.

Then Pai Ya changed the key and sang of love. The forest swayed like an ardent swain deep lost in thought. On high, like a haughty maiden, swept a cloud bright and fair; but passing, trailed long shadows on the ground, black like despair. Again the mode was changed; Pai Ya sang of war, of clashing steel and trampling steeds. And in the harp arose the tempest of Lung Men, the dragon rode the lightning, the thundering avalanche crashed through the hills. In ecstasy the Celestial Monarch asked Pai Ya wherein lay the secret of his victory. "Sire," he replied, "others have failed because they sang but of themselves. I left the harp to choose its theme, and knew not truly whether the harp had been Pai Ya or Pai Ya were the harp."

This story well illustrates the mystery of art appreciation. The masterpiece is a symphony played upon our finest feelings. True art is Pai Ya, and we the harp of Lung Men. At the magic touch of the beautiful the secret chords of our being are awakened, we vibrate and thrill in response to its call. Mind speaks to mind. We listen to the unspoken, we gaze upon the unseen. The master calls forth notes we know not of. Memories long forgotten all come back to us with a new significance. Hopes stifled by fear, yearnings that we dare not recognize, stand forth in new glory. Our mind is the canvas on which the artists lay their color; their pigments are our emotions; their chiaroscuro the light of joy, the shadow of sadness. The masterpiece is of ourselves, as we are of the masterpiece.

The sympathetic communion of minds necessary for art appreciation must be based on mutual concession. The spectator must cultivate the proper attitude for receiving the message, as the artist must know how to impart it. The tea master, Kobori-Enshiu, himself a *daimyo*, has left to us these memorable words: "Approach a great painting as thou wouldst approach a great prince." In order to understand a masterpiece, you must lay yourself low before it and await with bated breath its least utterance. An eminent Sung critic once made a charming confession. Said he: "In my young days I praised the master whose pictures I liked, but as my judgment matured I praised myself for liking what the masters had chosen to have me like." It is to be deplored that so few of us really take pains to study the moods of the masters. In our stubborn ignorance we refuse to render them this simple courtesy, and thus often miss the rich repast of beauty spread before our very eyes. A master has always something to offer, while we go hungry solely because of our own lack of appreciation.

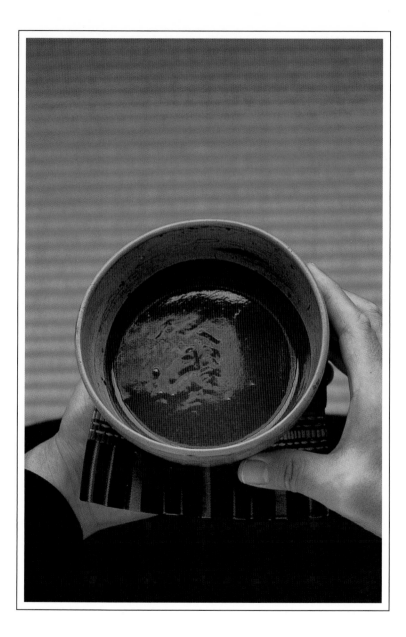

To the sympathetic a masterpiece becomes a living reality toward which we feel drawn in bonds of comradeship. The masters are immortal, for their loves and fears live in us over and over again. It is rather the soul than the hand, the man than the technique, which appeals to us—the more human the call the deeper is our response. It is because of this secret understanding between the master and ourselves that in poetry or romance we suffer and rejoice with the hero and heroine. Chikamatsu, our Japanese Shakespeare, has laid down as one of the first principles of dramatic composition the importance of taking the audience into the confidence of the author. Several of his pupils submitted plays for his approval, but only one of the pieces appealed to him. It was a play somewhat resembling the *Comedy of Errors,* in which twin brethren suffer through mistaken identity. "This," said Chikamatsu, "has the proper spirit of the drama, for it takes the audience into consideration. The public is permitted to know more than the actors. It knows where the mistake lies, and pities the poor figures on the board who innocently rush to their fate."

The great masters both of the East and the West never forgot the value of suggestion as a means for taking the spectator into their confidence. Who can contemplate a masterpiece without being awed by the immense vista of thought presented to our consideration? How familiar and sympathetic are they all; how cold in contrast the modern commonplaces! In the former we feel the warm outpouring of a man's heart; in the latter only a formal salute. Engrossed in his technique, the modern rarely rises above himself. Like the musicians who vainly invoked the Lung Men harp, he sings only of himself. His works may be nearer science, but are further from humanity. We have an old saying in Japan that a woman cannot love a man who is truly vain, for there is no crevice in his heart for love to enter and fill up. In art vanity is equally fatal to sympathetic feeling, whether on the part of the artist or the public.

Nothing is more hallowing than the union of kindred spirits in art. At the moment of meeting, the art lover transcends himself. At once he is and is not. He catches a glimpse of infinity, but words cannot voice his delight, for the eye has no tongue. Freed from the fetters of matter, his spirit moves in the rhythm of things. It is thus that art becomes akin to religion and ennobles mankind. It is this which makes a masterpiece something sacred. In the old days the veneration in which the Japanese held the work of the great artist was intense. The tea masters guarded their treasures with religious secrecy, and it was often necessary to open a whole series of boxes, one within another, before reaching the shrine itself—the silken wrapping within whose soft folds lay the holy of holies. Rarely was the object exposed to view, and then only to the initiated.

At the time when teaism was in the ascendency the Taiko's generals would be better satisfied with the present of a rare work of art than a large grant of territory as a reward of victory. Many of our favorite dramas are based on the loss and recovery of a noted masterpiece. For instance, in one play the palace of Lord Hosokawa, in which was preserved the celebrated painting of Dharuma by Sesson, suddenly takes fire through the negligence of the samurai in charge. Resolved at all hazards to rescue the precious painting, he rushes into the burning building and seizes the *kakemono*, only to find all means of exit cut off by the flames. Thinking only of the picture, he slashes open his body with his sword, wraps his torn sleeve about the Sesson and plunges it into the gaping wound. The fire is at last extinguished.

Among the smoking embers is found a half-consumed corpse, within which reposes the treasure uninjured by the fire. Horrible as such tales are, they illustrate the great value that we set upon a masterpiece, as well as the devotion of a trusted samurai.

We must remember, however, that art is of value only to the extent that it speaks to us. It might be a universal language if we ourselves were universal in our sympathies. Our finite nature, the power of tradition and conventionality, as well as our hereditary instincts, restrict the scope of our capacity for artistic enjoyment. Our very individuality establishes in one sense a limit to our understanding; and our aesthetic personality seeks its own affinities in the creations of the past. It is true that with cultivation our sense of art appreciation broadens, and we become able to enjoy many hitherto unrecognized expressions of beauty. But, after all, we see only our own image in the universe—our particular idiosyncrasies dictate the mode of our perceptions. The tea masters collected only objects which fell strictly within the measure of their individual appreciation.

One is reminded in this connection of a story concerning Kobori-Enshiu. Enshiu was complimented by his disciples on the admirable taste he had displayed in the choice of his collection. Said they, "Each piece is such that no one could help admiring. It shows that you had better taste than had Rikiu, for his collection could only be appreciated by one beholder in a thousand." Sorrowfully Enshiu replied: "This only proves how commonplace I am. The great Rikiu dared to love only those objects which personally appealed to him, whereas I unconsciously cater to the taste of the majority. Verily, Rikiu was one in a thousand among tea masters."

It is much to be regretted that so much of the apparent enthusiasm for art at the present day has no foundation in real feeling. In this democratic age of ours men clamor for what is popularly considered the best, regardless of their feelings. They want the costly, not the refined; the fashionable, not the beautiful. To the masses, contemplation of illustrated periodicals, the worthy product of their own industrialism, would give more digestible food for artistic enjoyment than the early Italians or the Ashikaga masters, whom they pretend to admire. The name of the artist is more important to them than the quality of the work. As a Chinese critic complained many centuries ago, "People criticize a picture by their ear." It is this lack of genuine appreciation that is responsible for the pseudo-classic horrors that today greet us wherever we turn.

Another common mistake is that of confusing art with archaeology. The veneration born of antiquity is one of the best traits in the human character, and fain would we have it cultivated to a greater extent. The old masters are rightly to be honored for opening the path to future enlightenment. The mere fact that they have passed unscathed through centuries of criticism and come down to us still covered with glory commands our respect. But we should be foolish indeed if we valued their achievement simply on the score of age. Yet we allow our historical sympathy to override our aesthetic discrimination. We offer flowers of approbation when the artist is safely laid in his grave. The nineteenth century, pregnant with the theory of evolution, has moreover created in us the habit of losing sight of the individual in the species. A collector is anxious to acquire specimens to illustrate a period or a school, and forgets that a single masterpiece can teach us more than any number of the mediocre products of a given period or school. We classify too much and enjoy too little. The sacrifice of the aesthetic to the so-called scientific method of exhibition has been the bane of many museums.

The claims of contemporary art cannot be ignored in any vital scheme of life. The art of today is that which really belongs to us: it is our own reflection. In condemning it we but condemn ourselves. We say that the present age possesses no art—who is responsible for this? It is indeed a shame that despite all our rhapsodies about the ancients we pay so little attention to our own possibilities. Struggling artists, weary souls lingering in the shadow of cold disdain! In our self-centered century, what inspiration do we offer them? The past may well look with pity at the poverty of our civilization; the future will laugh at the barrenness of our art. We are destroying art in destroying the beautiful in life. Would that some great wizard might from the stem of society shape a mighty harp whose strings would resound to the touch of genius.

Flowers

In the trembling grey of a spring dawn, when the birds were whispering in mysterious cadence among the trees, have you not felt that they were talking to their mates about the flowers? Surely with mankind the appreciation of flowers must have been coeval with the poetry of love. Where better than in a flower, sweet in its unconsciousness, fragrant because of its silence, can we image the unfolding of a virgin soul? The primeval man in offering the first garland to his maiden thereby transcended the brute. He became human in thus rising above the crude necessities of nature. He entered the realm of art when he perceived the subtle use of the useless.

In joy or sadness, flowers are our constant friends. We eat, drink, sing, dance, and flirt with them. We wed and christen with flowers. We dare not die without them. We have worshipped with the lily, we have meditated with the lotus, we have charged in battle array with the rose and the chrysanthemum. We have even attempted to speak in the language of flowers. How could we live without them? It frightens one to conceive of a world bereft of their presence. What solace do they not bring to the bedside of the sick, what a light of bliss to the darkness of weary spirits? Their serene tenderness restores to us our waning confidence in the universe even as the intent gaze of a beautiful child recalls our lost hopes. When we are laid low in the dust it is they who linger in sorrow over our graves.

Sad as it is, we cannot conceal the fact that in spite of our companionship with flowers we have not risen very far above the brute. Scratch the sheepskin and the wolf within us will soon show his teeth. It has been said that man at ten is an animal, at twenty a lunatic, at thirty a failure, at forty a fraud, and at fifty a criminal. Perhaps he becomes a criminal because he has never ceased to be an animal. Nothing is real to us but hunger, nothing sacred except our own desires. Shrine after shrine has crumbled before our eyes; but one altar forever is preserved, that whereon we burn incense to the supreme idol—ourselves. Our god is great, and money is his prophet! We devastate nature in order to make sacrifice to him. We boast that we have conquered matter and forget that it is matter that has enslaved us. What atrocities do we not perpetrate in the name of culture and refinement!

Tell me, gentle flowers, teardrops of the stars, standing in the garden, nodding your heads to the bees as they sing of the dews and the sunbeams, are you aware of the fearful doom that awaits you? Dream on, sway and frolic while you may in the gentle breezes of summer. Tomorrow a ruthless hand will close around your throats. You will be wrenched, torn asunder limb by limb, and borne away from your quiet homes. The wretch, she may be passing fair. She may say how lovely you are while her fingers are still moist with your blood. Tell me, will this be kindness? It may be your fate to be imprisoned in the hair of one whom you know to be heartless or to be thrust into the buttonhole of one who would not dare to look you in the face were you a man. It may even be your lot to be confined in some narrow vessel with only stagnant water to quench the maddening thrist that warns of ebbing life.

Flowers, if you were in the land of the Mikado, you might some time meet a dread personage armed with scissors and a tiny saw. He would call himself a Master of Flowers. He would claim the rights of a doctor and you would instinctively hate him, for you know a doctor always seeks to prolong the troubles of his victims. He would cut, bend, and twist you into those impossible positions which he thinks it proper that you should assume. He would contort your muscles and dislocate your bones like any osteopath. He would burn you with red-hot coals to stop your bleeding, and thrust wires into you to assist your circulation. He would diet you with salt, vinegar, alum, and sometimes, vitriol. Boiling water would be poured on your feet when you seemed ready to faint. It would be his boast that he could keep life within you for two or more weeks longer than would have been possible without his treatment. Would you not have preferred to have been killed at once when you were first captured?

What were the crimes you must have committed during your past incarnation to warrant such punishment in this?

The wanton waste of flowers among western communities is even more appalling than the way they are treated by eastern flower masters. The number of flowers cut daily to adorn the ballrooms and banquet tables of Europe and America, to be thrown away on the morrow, must be something enormous; if strung together they might garland a continent. Beside this utter carelessness of life, the guilt of the flower master becomes insignificant. He, at least, respects the economy of nature, selects his victims with careful foresight, and after death does honor to their remains. In the West the display of flowers seems to be a part of the pageantry of wealth—the fancy of a moment. Whither do they all go, these flowers, when the revelry is over? Nothing is more pitiful than to see a faded flower remorselessly flung upon a dung heap.

Why were the flowers born so beautiful and yet so hapless? Insects can sting, and even the meekest of beasts will fight when brought to bay. The birds whose plumage is sought to deck some bonnet can fly from its pursuer, the furred animal whose coat you covet for your own may hide at your approach. Alas! The only flower known to have wings is the butterfly; all others stand helpless before the destroyer. If they shriek in their death agony their cry never reaches our hardened ears. We are ever brutal to those who love and serve us in silence, but the time may come when, for our cruelty, we shall be deserted by these best friends of ours. Have you not noticed that the wild flowers are becoming scarcer every year? It may be that their wise men have told them to depart till man becomes more human. Perhaps they have migrated to heaven.

Much may be said in favor of him who cultivates plants. The man of the pot is far more humane than he of the scissors. We watch with delight his concern about water and sunshine, his feuds with parasites, his horror of frosts, his anxiety when the buds come slowly, his rapture when the leaves attain their luster. In the East the art of floriculture is a very ancient one, and the loves of a poet and his favorite plant have often been recorded in story and song. With the development of ceramics during the T'ang and Sung dynasties we hear of wonderful receptacles made to hold plants, not pots, but jewelled palaces. A special attendant was detailed to wait upon each flower and to wash its leaves with soft brushes made of rabbit hair. It has been written that the peony should be bathed by a handsome maiden in full costume, that a winter plum should be watered by a pale, slender monk. In Japan, one of the most popular of the No dances, the *Hachinoki*, composed during the Ashikaga period, is based upon the story of an impoverished knight, who, on a freezing night, in lack of fuel for a fire, cuts his cherished plants in order to entertain a wandering friar. The friar is in reality no other than Hojo-Tokiyori, the Haroun-Al-Raschid of our tales, and the sacrifice is not without its reward. This opera never fails to draw tears from a Tokyo audience even today.

Great precautions were taken for the preservation of delicate blossoms. Emperor Huensung, of the T'ang dynasty, hung tiny golden bells on the branches in his garden to keep off the birds. He it was who went off in the springtime with his court musicians to gladden the flowers with soft music. A quaint tablet, which tradition ascribes to Yoshit-sune, the hero of our Arthurian legends, is still ex-tant in one of the Japanese monasteries. It is a notice put up for the protection of a certain wonderful plum tree, and appeals to us with the grim humor of a warlike age. After referring to the beauty of the blossoms, the inscription says: "Whoever cuts a single branch of this tree shall forfeit a finger therefor." Would that such laws could be enforced nowadays against those who wantonly destroy flowers and mutilate objects of art!

Yet even in the case of pot flowers we are inclined to suspect the selfishness of man. Why take the plants from their homes and ask them to bloom mid strange surroundings? Is it not like asking the birds to sing and mate cooped up in cages? Who knows but that the orchids feel stifled by the artificial heat in your conservatories and hopelessly long for a glimpse of their own southern skies?

The ideal lover of flowers is he who visits them in their native haunts, like Tao Yuan Ming, who sat before a broken bamboo fence in converse with the wild chrysanthemum, or Lin Ho Ching, losing himself amid mysterious fragrance as he wandered in the twilight among the plum blossoms of the Western Lake. 'Tis said that Chow Mou Shiu slept in a boat so that his dreams might mingle with those of the lotus. It was this same spirit which moved the Empress Komio, one of our most renowned Nara sovereigns, as she sang: "If I pluck thee, my hand will defile thee. O Flower! Standing in the meadows as thou art, I offer thee to the Buddhas of the past, of the present, of the future."

However, let us not be too sentimental. Let us be less luxurious but more magnificent. Said Lao-tzu: "Heaven and earth are pitiless." Said Kobodaishi: "Flow, flow, flow, flow, the current of life is ever onward. Die, die, die, die, death comes to all." Destruction faces us wherever we turn. Destruction below and above, destruction behind and before. Change is the only eternal—why not as welcome death as life? They are but counterparts one of the other—the night and day of Brahma. Through the disintegration of the old, re-creation becomes possible. We have worshipped death, the relentless goddess of mercy, under many different names. It was the shadow of the all-devouring that the Gheburs greeted in the fire. It is the icy purism of the sword-soul before which Shinto-Japan prostrates herself even today. The mystic fire consumes our weakness, the sacred sword cleaves the bondage of desire. From our ashes springs the phoenix of celestial hope, out of the freedom comes a higher realization of manhood.

Why not destroy flowers if thereby we can evolve new forms ennobling the world idea? We only ask them to join in our sacrifice to the beautiful. We shall atone for the deed by consecrating ourselves to purity and simplicity. Thus reasoned the tea masters when they established the cult of flowers.

Anyone acquainted with the ways of our tea and flower masters must have noticed the religious veneration with which they regard flowers. They do not cull at random, but carefully select each branch or spray with an eye to the artistic composition they have in mind. They would be ashamed should they chance to cut more than were absolutely necessary. It may be remarked in this connection that they always associate the leaves, if there be any, with the flower, for their object is to present the whole beauty of plant life. In this respect, as in many others, their method differs from that pursued in Western countries. Here we are apt to see only the flower stems, heads, as it were, without body, stuck promiscuously into a vase.

When a tea master has arranged a flower to his satisfaction he will place it on the *tokonoma*, the place of honor in a Japanese room. Nothing else will be placed near it which might interfere with its effect, not even a painting, unless there be some special aesthetic reason for the combination. It rests there like an enthroned prince, and the guests or disciples on entering the room will salute it with a profound bow before making their addresses to the host. Drawings from masterpieces are made and published for the edification of amateurs. The amount of literature on the subject is quite voluminous. When the flower fades, the master tenderly consigns it to the river or carefully buries it in the ground. Monuments even are sometimes erected to their memory.

The birth of the art of flower arrangement seems to be simultaneous with that of teaism in the fifteenth century. Our legends ascribe the first flower arrangement to those early Buddhist saints who gathered the flowers strewn by the storm and, in their infinite solicitude for all living things, placed them in vessels of water. It is said that Soami, the great painter and connoisseur of the court of Ashikaga Yoshimasa, was one of the earliest adepts at it. Juko, the tea master, was one of his pupils, as was also Senno, the founder of the house of Ikenobo, a family as illustrious in the annals of flowers as was that of the Kanos in painting. With the perfecting of the tea ritual under Rikiu, in the latter part of the sixteenth century, flower arrangement also attains its full growth. Rikiu and his successors, the celebrated Ota-wuraka, Furuka-Oribe, Koyetsu, Kobori-Enshiu, Katagiri-Sekishiu, vied with each other in forming new combinations. We must remember, however, that the flower worship of the tea masters formed only a part of their aesthetic ritual, and was not a distinct religion by itself. A flower arrangement, like the other works of art in the tearoom, was subordinated to the total scheme of decoration. Thus Sekishiu ordained that white plum blossoms should not be made use of when snow lay in the garden. "Noisy" flowers were relentlessly banished from the tearoom. A flower arrangement by a tea master loses its significance if removed from the place for which it was originally intended, for its lines and proportions have been specially worked out with a view to its surroundings.

The adoration of the flower for its own sake begins with the rise of flower masters, toward the middle of the seventeenth century. It now becomes independent of the tearoom and knows no law save that that the vase imposes on it. New conceptions and methods of execution now become possible, and many were the principles and schools resulting therefrom. A writer in the middle of the last century said he could count over one hundred different schools of flower arrangement. Broadly speaking, these divide themselves into two main branches, the formalistic and the naturalesque. The formalistic schools, led by the Ikenobos, aimed at a classic idealism corresponding to that of the Kano-academicians. We possess records of arrangements by the early masters of this school which almost reproduce the flower paintings of Sansetsu and Tsunenobu. The naturalesque school, on the other hand, as its name implies, accepted nature as its model, only imposing such modifications of form as conduced to the expression of artistic unity. Thus we recognize in its works the same impulses which formed the Ukiyoe and Shijo schools of painting.

It would be interesting, had we time, to enter more fully than is now possible into the laws of composition and detail formulated by the various flower masters of this period, showing, as they would, the fundamental theories which governed Tokugawa decoration. We find them referring to the leading principle (heaven), the subordinate principle (earth), the reconciling principle (man), and any flower arrangement which did not embody these principles was considered barren and dead. They also dwelt much on the importance of treating a flower in its three different aspects, the formal, the semi-formal, and the informal. The first might be said to represent flowers in the stately costume of the ballroom, the second in the easy elegance of afternoon dress, the third in the charming deshabille of the boudoir.

Our personal sympathies are with the flower arrangements of the tea master rather than with those of the flower master. The former is art in its proper setting and appeals to us on account of its true intimacy with life. We should like to call this school the natural in contradistinction to the naturalesque and formalistic schools. The tea master deems his duty ended with the selection of the flowers, and leaves them to tell their own story. Entering a tea room in late winter, you may see a slender spray of wild cherries in combination with a budding camellia; it is an echo of departing winter coupled with the prophecy of spring. Again, if you go into a noon tea on some irritatingly hot summer day, you may discover in the darkened coolness of the *tokonoma* a single lily in a hanging vase; dripping with dew, it seems to smile at the foolishness of life.

A solo of flowers is interesting, but in a concerto with painting and sculpture the combination becomes entrancing. Sekishiu once placed some water-plants in a flat receptacle to suggest the vegetation of lakes and marshes, and on the wall above he hung a painting by Soami of wild ducks flying in the air. Shoha, another tea master, combined a poem on the beauty of solitude by the sea with a bronze incense burner in the form of a fisherman's hut and some wild flowers of the beach. One of the guests has recorded that he felt in the whole composition the breath of waning autumn.

Flower stories are endless. We shall recount but one more. In the sixteenth century the morning glory was as yet a rare plant with us. Rikiu had an entire garden planted with it, which he cultivated with assiduous care. The fame of his convolvuli reached the ear of the Taiko, and he expressed a desire to see them, in consequence of which Rikiu invited him to a morning tea at his house. On the appointed day Taiko walked through the garden, but nowhere could he see any vestige of the convolvulus. The ground had been leveled and strewn with fine pebbles and sand. With sullen anger the despot entered the tea-room, but a sight waited him there which completely restored his humor. On the *tokonoma*, in a rare bronze of Sung workmanship, lay a single morning glory—the queen of the whole garden!

In such instances we see the full significance of the flower sacrifice. Perhaps the flowers appreciate the full significance of it. They are not cowards like men. Some flowers glory in death—certainly the Japanese cherry blossoms do, as they freely surrender themselves to the winds. Anyone who has stood before the fragrant avalanche at Yoshino or Arashiyama must have realized this. For a moment they hover like bejewelled clouds and dance above the crystal streams; then, as they sail away on the laughing waters, they seem to say: "Farewell, O Spring! We are on to Eternity."

Tea Masters

In religion the future is behind us. In art the present is the eternal. The tea masters held that real appreciation of art is only possible to those who make of it a living influence. Thus they sought to regulate their daily life by the high standard of refinement which obtained in the tearoom. In all circumstances serenity of mind should be maintained, and conversation should be so conducted as never to mar the harmony of the surroundings. The cut and color of the dress, the poise of the body, and the manner of walking could all be made expressions of artistic personality. These

were matters not to be lightly ignored, for until
one has made himself beautiful he has no right to
approach beauty. Thus the tea master strove to be
something more than the artist—art itself. It was
the Zen of aestheticism. Perfection is everywhere
if we only choose to recognize it. Rikiu loved to
quote an old poem which says: "To those who
long only for flowers, fain would I show the full-
blown spring which abides in the toiling buds of
snow-covered hills."

Manifold indeed have been the contributions of
the tea masters to art. They completely revolution-
ized the classical architecture and interior decora-
tions, and established the new style which we have
described in the chapter of the tearoom, a style to
whose influence even the palaces and monasteries
built after the sixteenth century have all been subject. The many-sided Kobori-Enshiu has left no-
table examples of his genius in the Imperial villa of
Katsura, the castles of Najoya and Nijo, and the
monastery of Kohoan. All the celebrated gardens of
Japan were laid out by the tea masters. Our pottery
would probably never have attained its high quality
of excellence if the tea masters had not lent to it
their inspiration, the manufacture of the utensils

used in the tea ceremony calling forth the utmost expenditure of ingenuity on the part of our ceramists. The Seven Kilns of Enshiu are well known to all students of Japanese pottery. Many of our textile fabrics bear the names of tea masters who conceived their color or design. It is impossible, indeed, to find any department of art in which the tea masters have not left marks of their genius. In painting and lacquer it seems almost superfluous to mention the immense service they have rendered. One of the greatest schools of painting owes its origin to the tea master Honnami-Koyetsu, famed also as a lacquer artist and potter. Beside his works, the splendid creation of his grandson, Koho, and of his grand-nephews, Korin and Kenzan, almost fall into the shade. The whole Korin school, as it is generally designated, is an expression of teaism. In the broad lines of this school we seem to find the vitality of nature herself.

Great as has been the influence of the tea masters in the field of art, it is as nothing compared to that which they have exerted on the conduct of life. Not only in the usages of polite society, but also in the arrangement of all our domestic details, do we feel the presence of the tea masters. Many of our delicate dishes, as well as our way of serving food, are their inventions. They have taught us to dress only in garments of sober colors. They have instructed us in the proper spirit in which to approach flowers. They have given emphasis to our natural love of simplicity, and shown us the beauty of humility. In fact, through their teachings tea has entered the life of the people.

Those of us who know not the secret of properly regulating our own existence on this tumultuous sea of foolish troubles which we call life are constantly in a state of misery while vainly trying to appear happy and contented. We stagger in the attempt to keep our moral equilibrium, and see forerunners of the tempest in every cloud that floats on the horizon. Yet there is joy and beauty in the roll of the billows as they sweep outward toward eternity. Why not enter into their spirit, or, like Lieh-tzu, ride upon the hurricane itself?

He only who has lived with the beautiful can die beautifully. The last moments of the great tea masters were as full of exquisite refinement as had been their lives. Seeking always to be in harmony with the great rhythm of the universe, they were ever prepared to enter the unknown. The "Last Tea of

Rikiu" will stand forth forever as the acme of tragic grandeur.

Long had been the friendship between Rikiu and the Taiko-Hideyoshi, and high the estimation in which the great warrior held the tea master. But the friendship of a despot is ever a dangerous honor. It was an age rife with treachery, and men trusted not even their nearest kin. Rikiu was no servile courtier, and had often dared to differ in argument with his fierce patron. Taking advantage of the coldness which had for some time existed between the Taiko and Rikiu, the enemies of the latter accused him of being implicated in a conspiracy to poison the despot. It was whispered to Hideyoshi that the fatal potion was to be administered to him with a cup of the green beverage prepared by the tea master. With Hideyoshi suspicion was sufficient ground for instant execution, and there was no appeal from the will of the angry ruler. One privilege alone was granted to the condemned—the honor of dying by his own hand.

On the day destined for his self-immolation, Rikiu invited his chief disciples to a last tea ceremony. Mournfully at the appointed time the guests met at the portico. As they look into the garden path the trees seem to shudder, and in the rustling of their leaves are heard the whispers of homeless ghosts. Like solemn sentinels before the gates of Hades stand the grey stone lanterns. A wave of rare incense is wafted from the tearoom; it is the summons which bids the guests to enter. One by one they advance and take their places. In the *tokonoma* hangs a *kakemono*, a wonderful writing by an ancient monk dealing with the evanescence of all earthly things. The singing kettle, as it boils over the brazier, sounds like some cicada pouring forth his woes to departing summer. Soon the host enters the room. Each in turn is served with tea, and each in turn silently drains his cup, the host last of all. According to established etiquette, the chief guest now asks permission to examine the tea equipage. Rikiu places the various articles before them, with the *kakemono*. After all have expressed admiration of their beauty, Rikiu presents one of them to each of the assembled company as a souvenir. The bowl alone he keeps. "Never again shall this cup, polluted by the lips of misfortune, be used by man." He speaks, and breaks the vessel into fragments.

The ceremony is over; the guests with difficulty restraining their tears, take their last farewell and leave the room. One only, the nearest and dearest, is requested to remain and witness the end. Rikiu then removes his tea gown and carefully folds it upon the mat, thereby disclosing the immaculate white death robe which it had hitherto concealed. Tenderly he gazes on the shining blade of the fatal dagger, and in exquisite verse thus addresses it:

> Welcome to thee,
> O sword of eternity!
> Through Buddha
> And through Dharuma alike
> Thou hast cleft thy way.

With a smile upon his face Rikiu passed forth into the unknown.

Shambhala Classics

The Art of Worldly Wisdom, by Baltasar Gracián. Translated by Joseph Jacobs.

The Book of Five Rings, by Miyamoto Musashi. Translated by Thomas Cleary.

The Book of Tea, by Kakuzo Okakura.

Kabbalah: The Way of the Jewish Mystic, by Perle Epstein.

Narrow Road to the Interior and Other Writings, by Matsuo Bashō. Translated by Sam Hamill.

The Rumi Collection: An Anthology of Translations of Mevlâna Jalâluddin Rumi, edited by Kabir Helminski.

Seeking the Heart of Wisdom: The Path of Insight Meditation, by Joseph Goldstein and Jack Kornfield.

Siddhartha, by Hermann Hesse. Translated by Sherab Chödzin Kohn.

T'ai Chi Classics, translated with commentary by Waysun Liao.

The Tibetan Book of the Dead: The Great Liberation through Hearing in the Bardo, translated with commentary by Francesca Fremantle and Chögyam Trungpa.

When Things Fall Apart: Heart Advice for Difficult Times, by Pema Chödrön.